SWU-800- 006

UNIFORMS OF RUSSIAN ARMY DURING THE YEARS 1825-1855 VOL. 6

UNDER THE REIGN OF NICHOLAS I
EMPEROR OF RUSSIA BETWEEN 1825 TO 1855
INVALID, GARRISON, ARSENAL & OTHERS

From the Viskovatov's greatest work:
"Historical description of the clothing and
arms of the Russian Army"

English translation by Mark Conrad

SOLDIERSHOP PUBLISHING

AUTHOR

Aleksandr Vasilevich Viskovatov born 22 April (4 May New Style) 1804, died 27 February (11 March) 1858 in St. Petersburg, Russian military historian. He graduated from the 1st Cadet Corps and served in the artillery, the hydrographic depot of the Naval Ministry, and then in the Department of Military Educational Institutions. He mainly studied historical artifacts and the histories of military units. Viskovatov's greatest work was the Historical Description of the Clothing and Arms of the Russian Army.

NOTE ABOUT BOOK PRINTING BEFORE 1925

This book may contain text or images coming from a reproduction of a book published before 1925 (over seventy years ago). No effort has been made to modernize or standardize the spelling used in the original text, so this book may have occasional imperfections such as missing or blurred pages, poor pictures, errant marks, etc. that were either part of the original artifact, or were introduced by the scanning process. We believe this work is culturally important, and despite the imperfections, have elected to bring it back into print (digital and/or paper) as part of our continuing commitment to the preservation of printed works worldwide. We appreciate your understanding of the imperfections in the preservation process, and hope you enjoy this valuable book. Now this book is purpose re-built and is proof-read and re-type set from the original to provide an outstanding experience of reflowing text, also for an ebook reader. However Soldiershop publishing added, enriched, revised and overhauled the text, images, etc. of the cover and the book. Therefore, the job is now to all intents and purposes a derivative work, and the added, new and original parts of the book are the copyright of Soldiershop. On this second unpublished part of the book none of images or text may be reproduced in any format without the expressed written permission of Soldiershop. Almost many of the images of our books and prints are taken from original first edition prints or books that are no longer in copyright and are therefore public domain. We have been a specialized bookstore for a long time so we (and several friends antiquarian booksellers) have readily available a lot of ancient, historical and illustrated books not in copyright. Each of our prints, art designs or illustrations is either our own creation, or a fully digitally restoration by our computer artists, or non copyrighted images. All of our prints are "tagged" with a registered digital copyright. Soldiershop remains to disposition of the possible having right for all the doubtful sources images or not identifies.

ACKNOWLEDGEMENTS

A Special Thanks to NYPL and other institutions for their kindly permission to use some images of his archives, collections or books used in our book.

Title: **UNIFORMS OF RUSSIAN ARMY DURING THE YEARS 1825-1855. VOL. 6** -Under the reign of Nicholas I emperor of Russia between 1825-1855

By A.V.Viskovatov. Serie edit by Luca S. Cristini. First edition by Soldiershop. January 2019

Cover & Art Design: Luca S. Cristini. Plates re-colorations by Anna Cristini. ISBN code: 978-88-93274074

Published by Luca Cristini Editore, via Orio 35/4- 24050 Zanica (BG) ITALY. www.soldiershop.com

UNIFORMS
OF THE RUSSIAN ARMY
DURING THE YEARS
1825-1855
VOL. 6

UNDER THE REIGN OF NICHOLAS I EMPEROUR OF
RUSSIA BETWEEN 1825 AND 1855

*

INVALID, GARRISON, ARSENAL AND OTHERS

Portrait of Emperor Nicholas I in Austrian Uniform - Google Cultural Institute

HISTORICAL DESCRIPTION OF THE CLOTHING AND ARMS
OF THE RUSSIAN ARMY - A.V. VISKOVATOV
(First English translation by Mark Conrad)

Soldiershop is glad to presents the complete collection of the great job made by A.V. Viskovatov dedicated to the uniforms and weapons belonging from the first Zar and Russian emperors to the Russian army during the Napoleonic period, until 1860 about. The time we considered in this volume corresponds to the reigns of Nicholas I that was the Emperor of Russia from 1825 until 1855. He was also the King of Poland and Grand Duke of Finland. He is best known as a political conservative whose reign was marked by geographical expansion, repression of dissent, economic stagnation, poor administrative policies, a corrupt bureaucracy, and frequent wars that culminated in Russia's defeat in the Crimean War of 1853–56.

Our reprint in based on the original 19th century volumes. This part is distributed at now on six volumes.

Our new edition, the first ever published in English, both on paper and digital format, boasts a large number of color plates, many of them unpublished and re-coloured by our team of expert artists and scholars of uniformology. Each volume is based on 100 color plates or more, always accompanied by the original translated text which describes the subjects of the plates.

A unique work in its genre, a must have in any respecting collection!

Aleksandr Vasilevich Viskovatov born 22 April (4 May New Style) 1804, died 27 February (11 March) 1858 in St. Petersburg, Russian military historian. He graduated from the 1st Cadet Corps and served in the artillery, the hydrographic depot of the Naval Ministry, and then in the Department of Military Educational Institutions.

He mainly studied historical artifacts and the histories of military units. Viskovatov's greatest work was the Historical Description of the Clothing and Arms of the Russian Army (Vols. 1-30, St. Petersburg, 1841-62; 2nd ed. Vols. 1-34, St. Petersburg - Novosibirsk - Leningrad, 1899-1948). This work is based on a great quantity of archival documents and contains four thousand colored illustrations.

Viskovatov was the author of Chronicles of the Russian Army (Books 1-20, St. Petersburg, 1834-42) and Chronicles of the Russian Imperial Army (Parts 1-7, St. Petersburg, 1852). He collected valuable material on the history of the Russian navy which went into A Short Overview of Russian Naval Campaigns and General Voyages to the End of the XVII Century (St. Petersburg, 1864; 2nd edition Moscow, 1946). Together with A.I. Mikhailovskii-Danilevskii he helped prepare and create the Military Gallery in the Winter Palace.

He wrote the historical military inscriptions for the walls of the Hall of St. George in the Great Palace of the Kremlin. (From the article in the Soviet Military Encyclopedia.)

CONTENTS

*

Preface pag. 5

HISTORICAL DESCRIPTION OF THE CLOTHING AND ARMS OF THE RUSSIAN ARMY

Étape, and Salt Invalid Commands; Garrison Artillery, Garrison Engineers; Military-Labor, Arsenal, and Park Companies of the Engineer Administration; Battalions and Companies of the Military Settlements Administration, and Arrest Companies 1825-1855

CHANGES IN THE UNIFORMS AND EQUIPMENT OF TEMPORARY FORCES FROM 1801 TO 1825.

23 - DISTRICT INVALID COMMANDS (*UEZDNYYA INVALIDNYYA KOMANDY*).

11 February 1826 - Lower ranks in District Invalid commands are given single-breasted **coats** (*mundiry*) instead of double-breasted, grey in color as previously, with nine flat buttons in front, and pants with knee gaiters (*kragi*) are replaced with long **pants** the same color as the coat, with yellow piping on the side seams (Illus. 540). Officers keep their dark-green coats, but single-breasted as for lower ranks, with grey pants with yellow piping on the side seams (Illus. 541). Lower ranks at all times, and company-grade officers only when wearing the sash, are ordered to wear black cloth **half-gaiters** (*polushtiblety*), fastened with five or six small brass buttons. Along with this change, the horizontal **belt for the knapsack** (*poperechnyi rantsevyi remen*) is to be between the two lower buttons on the front of the coat, while the **greatcoat** (*shinel*) is carried on the knapsack (*ranets*) rolled into a tube in its special oilskin case made of raven's-duck (*ravenduchnaya kleenka*) [196].

26 June 1826 - Officers and lower ranks are ordered to have completely grey **pants**, without piping (Illus. 542) [197].

15 September 1826 - Lower ranks who have completed the regulation number of years of faultless service and voluntarily remain on active duty are to wear a gold **galloon chevron** (*nashivka iz galuna*) on the left sleeve, as related above for Grenadier regiments. [198].

1 January 1827 - Officers' epaulettes, in addition to any number, are to have little gold forged and stamped stars as **rank distinctions** in the same form and scheme as described above for Grenadier and other regiments of Army infantry [199].

24 March 1828 - The **coats** of lower ranks are not to be tailored with cinches [200].

24 April 1828 - There are the same **changes in uniforms and accouterments** as described above for Garrison regiments and battalions, with the only difference being that in District Invalid commands the small grenades on shakos are ordered have a single flame instead of three, with the cut-out number of the battalion to which the command is assigned (Illus. 543) [201].

20 August 1829 - District Invalid commands assigned to Line battalions of the Separate Caucasus Corps are to have **sheepskin headdresses** instead of shakos, identical to those prescribed for these battalions but with a single-flame grenade (Illus. 544) [202].

2 October 1829 - **District Invalid commands** are ordered to have:

   a) An entirely dark-green coat with a yellow number on the shoulder straps, corresponding to the Internal Guard battalion to which the command is assigned.

   b) Dark-green pants.

   c) Tin buttons on the cloth half-gaiters.

   d) Crossbelt, swordbelt, knapsack straps, musket sling, greatcoat strap, and mess-tin strap, and also frizzen covers of white Russian leather, are all to be of the patterns for Jäger regiments, blackened with black polish.

   e) Brass numbers on the pouch lid, following the pattern for Jäger reg., the same as prescribed for the shako grenades. Other items of uniform and armaments remain unchanged (Illus. 545) [203].

20 August 1830 - Officers' rapiers (*shpagi*) are replaced with **half-sabers** (*polusabli*) of the same pattern confirmed at this time for Grenadier and other regiments of Army infantry [204].

2 June 1832 - (Sic, should be 8 June - M.C.) Officers are permitted to wear **moustaches** [205].

3 January 1833 - **Cloth half-gaiters** (*polushtiblety*) are abolished for company-grade officers and lower ranks , as are sword knots for non-commissioned officers and drummers. **Covers** for shakos and cartridge pouches are abolished for non-commissioned officers and privates [206].

20 January 1833 - **Covers** for shakos are restored as before [207].

20 February 1833 - All combatant ranks are given new pattern **summer pants** or **breeches** (*pantalony ili bryuki*), without buttons or integral spats (Illus. 546) [208].

22 February 1833 - Field and company-grade officers are not to use the hat, but rather wear the **shako** at all times [209].

29 January 1834 - In order to introduce uniformity to shako **chin straps**, it is ordered that they be of black Russian leather, 1/2 vershok (7/8 inch) wide, sewn to the left side of the shako underneath the lower reinforcement strap, flush, and fastened by a button sewn onto the right side of the shako above the lower reinforcement [210].

26 September 1834 - Lower ranks are directed to wear the **knapsack** on two belts lying crosswise over the chest [211].

20 August 1835 - A directive regarding officers' **knapsacks** (*rantsy*) is issued , the same as set forth above for Line battalions [212].

31 January 1836 - Lower ranks' **greatcoats** (*shineli*) are to have nine buttons instead of ten: six along the front opening, two on the shoulder straps, and one on the flap behind [213].

27 April 1836 - The lower **pompons** (*repeiki*) are to be lined with black leather [214].

15 July 1837 - Approval is given to the new pattern of officers' **sash**, identical to that introduced at this time for Army infantry regiments and described above for Grenadier regiments [215].

17 December 1837 - Approval is given to a new pattern of officers' **epaulettes**, identical to those introduced at this time for Grenadier regiments and described above [216].

4 January 1839 - Field and company-grade officers are not to have any bows or bands on the front of their **pants** or **trousers**. These are to be worn completely plain in the manner prescribed for lower ranks [217].

16 March 1839 - Lower ranks' **pouch-belts** and **sword-belts** (*perevyazi i portupei*) are to be 1 1/2 vershoks (2 3/5 inches)wide, while **drummers' crossbelts** are as before, 2 1/2 vershoks (4 2/5 inches) wide [218].

16 October 1840 - Lower combatant ranks who voluntarily remain in service after serving out the regulation period for retirement are to be given, for subsequent service, sewn-on silver galloon **chevrons** for the left sleeve, after every five years service [219].

23 January 1841 - The capes (*bolshie vorotniki*) of officers' **greatcoats** are to be 1 arshin (28 inches) long as measured from the lower edge of the collar (*malyi vorotnik*) [220].

19 March 1841 - Sword belts (*portupei*) are taken away from privates, and it is directed that they only have **crossbelts** (*perevyazi*) with a frog for the bayonet that in full parade dress (*polnaya paradnaya forma*) is buttoned to the pouch and worn over the left shoulder, while in half-dress (*poluforma*), when personnel are without pouches, it is worn over the right shoulder [221].

26 November 1842 - Officers and lower ranks of District Invalid commands in the Separate Caucasus Corps are ordered to wear **forage caps** instead of the sheepskin headdress until such time as a new uniform is established. The forage caps prescribed for all Invalid commands are of dark-green cloth without any other colors [222].

8 April 1843 - Officers and lower ranks, except in commands in the Caucasus Corps, are given a new pattern **shako**, 4 3/4 vershoks (8 1/3 inches) high and curving slightly inward toward the bottom. Along with this, for all commands trim on the shoulder straps (*nashivki na plechevye pogony*) of sergeants (*feldfebeli*), non-commissioned officers (*unter-ofitsery*), and lance-corporals (*yefreitory*) is established following the same scheme as for these ranks in Infantry and Jäger regiments [223].

10 May 1843 - The covers of the **cartridge-pouches** (*patronnyya sumki*) are not to have any break on top (*bez pereloma vverkhu*), and are to measure (with the cover sewn onto the body of the pouch): length — 5 vershoks (8 3/4 inches), width at the top edge — 5 1/2 vershoks (9 5/8 inches), width at the bottom edge — 6 vershoks (10 1/2 inches) [224].

2 January 1844 - Officers are to have a **cockade** on the front of their forage caps, of the same colors as prescribed for cockades on officers' hats [225].

9 May 1844 - Officers and lower combatant ranks are given **helmets** in place of shakos, identical to those confirmed at this time for Internal Guard battalions but with a single-flame grenade (Illus. 547) [226].

4 January 1845 - Officers' **helmets** are to have a metallic cockade on the right side under the chin-scales [227].

23 June 1846 - Upon the introduction of percussion-lock weapons, the description for fitting the **firing-cap pouch** is approved as detailed above for Grenadier regiments [228].

8 August 1846 - District Invalid commands of the the **Separate Caucasus Corps** are prescribed the new uniforms and equipment confirmed at this time, and described in detail above, for Grenadier regiments [229].

9 and 25 November 1849 - The fitting of **helmets** is confirmed as described in detail above for Grenadier regiments [230].

17 January 1851 - Approval is given to the descriptions for folding up and turning back the skirts of the **greatcoat** as laid out above for Grenadier regiments [231].

8 July 1851 - Frizzen covers (*polunagalishcha*) are abolished and approval given to the patterns and descriptions of the **drum**, **water flask**, **greatcoat strap**, **sword-belt**, **crossbelt**, and **cover for the firing nipple** of percussion weapons, all as presented above for Grenadier regiments [232].

24 - ÉTAPE INVALID COMMANDS (*ETAPNYYA INVALIDNYYA KOMANDY*).

Changes in the uniforms, weapons, and accouterments of **Étape Invalid commands** were the same as for District Invalid commands except that on **21 June 1837** there were the following directives regarding *Horse-Étape commands:*

a.) Wearing the same uniform as personnel on foot, lower ranks' pants are to be lined with leather in the manner of cavalry riding trousers (*reituzy*). Lower ranks are to have a saber on a black sword belt and a holder for one pistol on a strap worn around the neck; pikes—of the pattern for lancers but without pennants; pouches and belts for them—black; saddle cloths (*val'trapy*)—of dark-green cloth, without monogram or piping; valises—of grey cloth; saddles—as for light cavalry; bridles—similar to cossacks' (Illus. 550) [233].

b.) Company-grade officers, wearing the same uniform as officers in foot commands, have cavalry sabers; likewise cavalry sword belts, of black Russian leather, with silver fittings (Illus. 551), and horse furniture as for lower ranks [224].

c.) Lower ranks as well as officers have shakos always in covers [225].

27 April 1838 - Officers of Horse-Étape commands are ordered to have **spurs** [226].

9 May 1844 - In Horse-Étape commands shakos are replaced by **helmets**, the same as for foot commands, without cockades, and from **4 January 1845**—with **cockades** for officers (Illus. 552) [237].

25 - SALT INVALID COMMANDS (*SOLYANYYA INVALIDNYYA KOMANDY*).

Changes in the uniforms, weapons, and accouterments of **Salt Invalid commands** were the same as for District Invalid commands with the only difference being that Salt commands had the Cyrillic letter S ("C") on the shako grenade, epaulettes, and shoulder straps [238].

26 - MOBILE INVALID COMPANIES (*PODVIZHNYYA INVALIDNYYA ROTY*).

Changes in the uniforms, weapons, and accouterments of **Mobile Invalid commands** were the same as for District Invalid commands with only the following differences :

11 February 1826 - **Coats** and **pants** for officers as well as lower ranks remain dark green without piping (Ills. 553 and 554), unlike in District commands (except for officers' coats) where uniforms were grey. **Numbers** on shako grenades in Mobile Invalid companies, and also on epaulettes and shoulder straps, were those assigned to the companies [239].

2 October 1829 - For **Mobile Invalid companies** at hospitals, the 2nd Cadet Corps, the Provisioning Department, and the various institutions in Gatchina, it was ordered:

a.) To have forage caps instead of shakos, of dark-green cloth, a band of the same, and on that the cut-out company number backed by yellow cloth (Illus. 555).

b.) To have jackets (*kurtki*) instead of uniform coats (of the pattern for lower-rank noncombatant master craftsmen), of dark-green cloth with the same collar, cuffs, and shoulder straps. On the shoulder straps is the cut-out company number in yellow (Illus. 555).

c.) There are no accouterments for weapons [240].

In other commands the uniform, armament, and accouterments remained the same.

30 July 1853 - For Mobile Invalid companies at military hospitals, **knapsacks** with **water flasks** and **greatcoat cases** were withdrawn, and were left only for the exact number of personnel who made up hospital cadres [241].

27 - GARRISON ARTILLERY (*GARNIZONNAYA ARTILLERIYA*).

11 February 1826 - Officers and combatant lower ranks (sergeants (*fel'dfebeli*), fireworkers (*feierverkery*), cannoneers (*kanoniry*), gun handlers (*gandlangery*), and drummers (*barabanshchiki*)) of Garrison Artillery companies and half-companies are given **single-breasted coats** (*mundiry*) in place of the double-breasted ones, of the style prescribed at this time for all Army and Garrison infantry troops, with, as before, red piping and white buttons. Also given are long dark-green pants with red piping on the side seams. Lower ranks at all times, and company-grade officers only when in formation with sashes, are ordered to wear black cloth **half-gaiters** (*polushtiblety*) under these pants and over the boots, fastened with five or six small white buttons (Illus. 556). Along with this change, the horizontal belt for the **knapsack** is to be between the two lower buttons on the front of the coat, while the **greatcoat** is carried on the knapsack rolled into a tube in its special oilskin case made of raven's-duck (*ravenduchnaya kleenka*). These changes in uniform are extended to Arsenals with the difference that their personnel (officers, sergeants, and fireworkers) have yellow buttons, shako badges, and shoulder straps while Garrison Artillery companies and half-companies have white buttons and shako badges and dark-green shoulder straps piped red [242].

(*Note: *Feierverker*, from German *Feuerwerker*. In the Russian artillery, non-commissioned officers were titled "fireworkers" in deference to their gunnery and artificer skills. Note also that here "non-commissioned officers" are what western armies would call sergeants, and "sergeants/*fel'dfebeli*" are what would be called sergeants major - M.C.)

10 June 1826 - For Garrison Artillery companies **shoulder straps** on coats and greatcoats are ordered to be of red chancellery (*kantselyarnoe*) cloth (Illus. 557), and along with this the color red is prescribed for the cloth field of officers' epaulettes [243].

24 August 1826 - For Garrison Artillery companies **shoulder straps** on greatcoats are ordered to be of madder red cloth (*iz krasnago, krapovago sukna*) [244].

13 September 1826 - The following uniforms are approved for personnel in local Arsenals, Powder works, and Laboratory comp.:

a) For **Arsenal sergeants and fireworkers**—the same uniforms as for Foot Field Artillery , but with dark-green cuff flaps, piped red; yellow shoulder straps with red initial Cyrillic letters (in the St.-Petersburg Arsenal—*P.A.*, in the Kiev Arsenal—*K.A.*, in the Bryansk. Arsenal—*B.A.*, and the Kazan Arsenal—*Ka.A.*; shakos without cords, with a chin strap instead of chin-scales, and with a brass badge of two crossed cannons, under which is a small single-flame grenade (Illus. 558).

b) For **Arsenal master craftsmen**—dark-green jacket (*kurtka*) without tails or piping, with black collar and cuffs; dark-green cuff flaps; red piping on the collar, cuffs, and flaps; with the same buttons (single row) and shoulder straps as the preceding personnel; grey winter pants (*bryuki*), but in summer of Flemish linen; dark-green forage cap with a visor, black band, red pipings, and yellow letters, the same as prescribed for the shoulder straps (Illus. 559)/

c) For **Laboratory fireworkers**—the same uniform as for Arsenal fireworkers, but black shoulder straps instead of yellow, piped red, and forage caps instead of shakos, of dark-green cloth with a visor, black band, and red piping on the band. On the shoulder straps and cap band are red cut-out company numbers and the Cyrillic letter *L*. (Illus. 560).

d) For **non-commissioned officers in Powder works** (*Porokhovye zavody*)—the same uniform as for Arsenal non-commissioned officers but with white distinctions instead of yellow (Illus. 561), and with red initial Cyrillic letters: in the Okhtensk works—*O.Z.*; the Shostensk—*Sh.Z.*; the Kazan—*K.Z.*

e) For non-commissioned officers and privates of **non-settled labor companies at the Okhtensk Powder Works**—the same uniform as for Arsenal non-commissioned officers but with the grenade on the shako not having any cannons, and with the appropriate letters on shoulder straps and forage caps (Illus. 562).

f) For **supply-train non-commissioned officers** (*furshtatskie unter-ofitsery*) at the Okhtensk Powder Works—grey coats with black piping, brass buttons, and yellow shoulder straps on which are cut-out red letters; silver galloon on the collar and cuffs; grey pants with black piping and leather reinforcement on the lower leg; grey forage cap with a visor, black piping, and yellow cut-out letters; infantry short sword (*tesak*) on a white sword belt (Illus. 563).

g) For **supply-train personnel** (*furleity*) of this powder works—the same uniform as for the preceding, but without galloon or short sword (Illus. 563) [245].

15 September 1826 - Lower ranks who have completed the regulation number of years of faultless service and have the right to be discharged but who voluntarily remain on active duty are to wear **gold galloon** (*nashivka iz zolotago galuna*) sewn onto the left sleeve above and in addition to the yellow tape (*bason*) prescribed on 29 March 1825 [246].

1 January 1827 - Officers' **epaulettes** are to have small forged and stamped silver stars as rank distinctions, of the same pattern and scheme as for other infantry troops: on gold epaulettes—in silver, and on silver epaulettes—in gold [247].

14 December 1827 - The sewn-on **galloon** established for lower ranks on 15 September 1826 is ordered to be gold to accompany yellow buttons, and silver to accompany white buttons [248].

24 March 1828 - The **coats** of lower ranks are not to be tailored with cinches [249].

24 April 1828 - The Garrison Artillery is given a new pattern **shako**, identical with those introduced at this time for other infantry troops, except without cords for lower ranks:

a) For Garrison Artillery companies—with black chin straps and a badge depicting two crossed cannons, under which is a small single-flame grenade; for lower ranks this badge is of white tin, and for officers—silvered (Illus. 564).

b) For Local and Mobile Arsenals and Laboratory companies—with brass chin-scales and the same badge as for Garrison Artillery companies, but yellow (Illus. 565).

c) For Powder works—as for Garrison Artillery companies.

Along with the change in the shako there were the following changes:

1.) The width of the **crossbelt** (*perevyaz'*) in Garrison Artillery companies and the **swordbelt** (*portupei*) is stipulated as 2 vershoks (3 1/2 inches), of **knapsack shoulder belts** (*rantsevye plechevye remni*) — 1 1/2 vershoks (2 5/8 inches), and of the **belt across the chest** (*nagrudnyi remen*) — 1 1/8 vershoks (2 inches).

2.) Knapsacks (*rantsy*) (in Garrison Artillery companies and Mobile Arsenals) are to be of calfskin as before but with the addition of black leather trim. The knapsack is prescribed to be 9 vershoks (15 3/4 inches) wide, 8 vershoks (14 inches) tall, and 2 vershoks (3 1/2 inches) deep. The length of the cover from the upper edge is 6 vershoks (10 1/2) inches.

3.) All non-combatant non-commissioned officers are given dark-green **frock coats** (*syurtuki*) with a single row of buttons and the same collar, cuffs, and shoulder straps as for combatant personnel. **Pants**, however, are grey with red piping on the side seams. Non-combatant craftsmen (*masterovye*) of the lower ranks are to wear grey cloth **jackets** (*kurtki*) modeled on the coat, with the same **pants** as for the non-combatants above [250].

10 August 1829 - In the Caucasus and Georgia Garrison Artillery Districts the shako is replaced by a black **sheepskin shapka headdress** like that introduced at this time for other infantry troops of the Separate Caucasus Corps, but without pompons, and with the same badge as was on the shako (Illus.566) [251].

16 December 1829 - Field and company-grade officers of the Garrison Artillery are to have the cuffs on their **frock coats** (*syurtuki*) are changed from black to dark green as previously, with red piping [252].

March 1830 - Field and company-grade officers and combatant lower ranks of the Garrison Artillery are ordered to have **buttons** with the raised image of two crossed cannons, with numbers, or numerals and Cyrillic letters: in Garrison Artillery companies—with the number designating the brigade (Illus. 561a); in the St.-Petersburg Arsenal—with the letters *P.A.* (Illus. 567b), in the Kiev Arsenal—*K.A.* (Illus. 567c); in the Bryansk Arsenal—*B.A.* (Illus. 567d), in the Kazan Arsenal—*Ka.A.* (Illus. 567e); in the Okhtensk Powder Works—*O.Z.* (Illus. 567f); in the Shostensk Powder Works—*Sh.Z.* (Illus. 567g), in the Kazan Powder Works—*K.Z.* (Illus. 567h); in Mobile Arsenals—the Arsenal number and the letters *P.A.* (for "*Podvizhnyi Arsenal*") (Illus. 567i); in Laboratory companies—the company number and the letter *L.* (Illus. 567k) [253].

8 June 1832 - Officers are permitted to wear **moustaches** [254].

13 October 1832 - Lower ranks of Arms factories (*Oruzheinye zavody*) are ordered to have, on the **shoulder straps** of coats, jackets, and greatcoats, and on the bands of forage caps, cut-outs of distinguishing Cyrillic letters, backed by yellow cloth: in the Sestroretsk Factory—*S.Z.*, in the Tula Factory—*T.Z.*, and in the Izhevsk Factory—*I.Z.* [255].

3 January 1833 - **Cloth half-gaiters** are abolished throughout the Garrison Artillery, as well as **short swords, pouchs, and pouch belts** in Garrison Artillery companies (Illus. 568) [256].

20 February 1833 - All personnel with with white summer pants with buttons and integral spats have these replaced by **trousers** without buttons or integral spats (Illus. 569) [257].

22 February 1833 - Officers of the Garrison Artillery, except those in the capitals, are not to use the hat, but rather use the **shako** at all times [258].

27 July 1833 - For uniformity with other troops, the Garrison Artillery is ordered to have their previous **badges** on the shako, of two crossed cannons over a grenade, but this last of a size capable of accomodating numerals and Cyrillic letters: in Garrison Artillery companies—the brigade number; in the St.-Petersburg Arsenal—the letters *P.A.*, in the Kiev Arsenal—*K.A.*, in the Bryansk Arsenal—*B.A.*, in the Kazan Arsenal—*Ka.A.*, in the Okhtensk Powder Works—*O.Z.*, in the Shostensk Powder Works—*Sh.Z.*, in the Kazan Powder Works—*K.Z.*, in Laboratory companies—the company number and the letter *L.*; in Mobile Arsenals—the Arsenal number and the letters *P.A.* [259].

5 November 1833 - Instead of a rapier (*shpaga*), officers of Garrison Artillery are ordered to wear **half-sabers** (*polusabli*) as prescribed for infantry officers (Illus. 570) [260].

4 January 1834 - Instead of black **shoulder straps**, lower ranks in Laboratory companies are ordered to have dark-green with red piping and a red numeral signifying the company. The field of officers' epaulettes are also ordered to be dark green, with a gold numeral [261].

29 January 1834 - In order to introduce uniformity to shako **chin straps**, it is ordered that they be of black Russian leather, 1/2 vershok (7/8 inch) wide, sewn to the left side of the shako underneath the lower reinforcement strap, flush, and fastened by a button sewn onto the right side of the shako above the lower reinforcement [262].

26 September 1834 - Lower ranks in Garrison Artillery companies are directed to wear the **knapsack** on two belts lying crosswise over the chest (Illus. 571) [263].

(**13 October 1834** - The commander of the Kronstadt Artillery Garrison received an expression of HIGHEST gratitude for the zeal and efforts he showed in uniforming and training lower ranks of the Instructional Garrison Artillery Detachment (*Uchebnaya Garnizonnaya Artilleriiskaya komanda*) located in Kronstadt (*Russkii Invalid*, No. 267, 22 October 1834, page 1066).)

20 August 1835 - It is ordered that officers of Garrison Artillery companies and Mobile Arsenals wear the **knapsack** using only two shoulder belts, without any cross strap or chest strap, and for lower ranks a **linen case** (*kholshchevyi chekhol*) or pocket (*karman*) for the forage cap is to be put on the outside of the knapsack on the side that lies on the soldier's back, these cases being made from the linings of wornout coats [264].

31 January 1836 - The lower ranks' **greatcoat** (*shinel*) is to have nine buttons instead of ten, namely: six along the front opening, two on the shoulder straps, and one on the flaps behind [265].

27 April 1836 - **Lower pompons** (*repeiki*) are to be lined with black leather [266].

15 July 1837 - A new pattern of officers' **sash** is approved, identical to that introduced at this time in the regiments of army infantry and cavalry and described above [267].

17 December 1837 - A new pattern of officers' **epaulette** is approved, identical with that introduced at this time for other infantry troops, i.e. with the additon of a fourth twist of braid [268].

4 January 1839 - The **pants** and **trousers** of field and company-grade officers are not to have any bows or bands on the front, but are to have them completely plain in the manner prescribed for lower ranks [269].

16 March 1839 - Lower ranks' **swordbelts** are to be 1 1/2 vershoks (2 5/8 inches) wide [270].

16 October 1840 - Lower ranks who have earned the right to discharge on indefinite leave but who voluntarily remain on active service after completing the regulation term of service are to be given gold or silver (according to the color of the buttons) galloon **chevrons** (*shevrony*) to be sewn onto the left sleeve, one for every five years of extra service [271].

23 January 1841 - The capes of officers' **greatcoats** are to be 28 inches long as measured from the lower edge of the collar [272].

26 November 1842 - Until a new uniform is approved, the Caucasus and Georgia Districts of Garrison Artillery are ordered to wear **forage caps** in place of the sheepskin headdress (*shapka*) [273].

16 January 1843 - To distinguish lower ranks who have committed transgressions and undergone punishments, thin **sewn-on grey and black cords** are established, on the same basis as related above for Line battalions [274].

21 February 1843 - The aforementioned grey and black **cords** are ordered to be worn on the shoulder straps below the cut-out number, on greatcoats as well as on dress coats [275].

8 April 1843 - A new model **shako** is approved for officers and lower ranks of the Garrison Artillery now wearing shakos (except the Caucasus and Georgia Districts). These new shakos are 4 3/4 vershoks (8 1/3 inches) high and curve slightly inward toward the bottom. (Illus. 572).

Along with this trim sewn onto the **shoulder straps** of sergeants and fireworkers is established, on the same basis as prescribed for these ranks in the Field Artillery [276].

2 January 1844 - Officers are to have a **cockade** on the cap band of the forage cap, identical to that introduced at this time for other branches (Illus. 573) [277].

9 May 1844 - In the Garrison Artillery shakos are replaced by **helmets** (*kaski*) identical to those established at this time for other infantry troops, without a plume and with the same badge as was on the shako (Illus. 574 and 575) [278].

20 May 1844 - With the general allocation of **forage-cap** particulars throughout the Army, lower ranks of the Garrison Artillery keep their caps as before—dark green with a black cloth band piped red along the edges, and with cut-out company numerals and a Cyrillic letter, backed by yellow cloth: for Garrison Artillery Company N° 1—*1.R.*, for Company N° 2—*2.R.*, for Laboratory Company N° 3—*3.L.*, etc. Arsenals and Powder works keep their initial letters as before, the same as prescribed for shoulder straps. Officers have the same forage caps but without numbers or letters and with a visor [279].

4 January 1845 - Officers' **helmets** are to have, on the right side under the chin-scales, a cockade, of the pattern for the cockade used on hats (Illus. 576) [280].

6 February 1846 - The Garrison Artillery, Laboratory companies, and Arsenals are ordered to have **helmets** with a single-flame grenade above two crossed cannons (Illus. 577) [281].

4 November 1846 - **Commanders of Fortress Artillery administrations** who belong to the Field Artillery are ordered to wear the same uniform prescribed for the Garrison Artillery officer under them, except that Commanders of such administrations, not belonging to any individual company, have epaulettes with a blank silver field [282].

19 May 1847 - With the new general directive concerning the colors for **forage caps** within the War Department (*Voennoe* *vedomstvo*, i.e. the entire army — M.C.), clerks (*pisarya*), medics (*feldshera*), and other lower ranks of the Garrison Artillery are prescribed caps with of the following colors:

a.) Laboratory companies—dark-green caps, without visors for fireworkers, but for privates with both visor and chin strap; black band with red piping around both edges and the cut-out company number and the Cyrillic letter L., backed by yellow cloth; red piping around the top of the cap.

b.) Power works and Arms factories—dark-green caps, without visors for fireworkers, but for privates with both visor and chin strap; black band with red piping around both edges and cut-out Cyrillic letters backed by yellow cloth:

Powder Works:

Okhtensk . . . . . . O. Z.

Shostensk . . . . . .Sh. Z.

Kazan . . . . .K. Z.

Arms Factories:

Sestroretsk . . . . . S. Z.

Tula . . . . .T. Z.

Izhevsk . . . . I. Z.

Red piping around the top of the cap.

c.) Local Arsenals—dark-green caps, without visors for fireworkers, but for privates with both visor and chin strap; black band with red piping around both edges and cut-out Cyrillic letters backed by yellow cloth: St.-Petersburg Arsenal—P.A., Bryansk—B.A., Kazan—Ka.A., and Kiev—K.A. Red piping around the top of the cap.

d.) Mobile Arsenals—dark-green caps, without visors for fireworkers, but for privates with both visor and chin strap; black band with red piping around both edges and the cut-out Arsenal number and the Cyrillic letters P.A., backed by yellow cloth; red piping around the top of the cap.

e.) Arms factories—dark-green caps, without visors for fireworkers, but for privates with both visor and chin strap; black band with red piping around both edges; red piping around the top of the cap.

f.) Master craftsmen of Laboratory companies, Powder works, Arms factories, and Arsenals—the same pattern cap as for low ranks of these units; a fatigue cap (*rabochaya shapka*), however, of grey cloth.

g.) The Technical, Farrier, and Powder Schools—dark-green caps, without visors for fireworkers, but for lower ranks with both visor and chin strap; black band with red piping around both edges and cut-out letters backed by yellow cloth: Technical School—T.Sh. ("*Tekhnicheskaya Shkola*"); Farrier School—K.Sh. ("*Konoval'naya Shkola*"); Powder School—P.Sh. ("*Porokhovaya Shkola*"); red piping around the top of the cap.

h.) For clerks (*pisarya*), ordnance workers (*tseikhdinery*), and ordnance clerks (*tseikhshreibery*) in Mobile Reserve parks, local Artillery parks, Artillery Garrisons, Laboratories, local Arsenals, Mobile Arsenals, Powder works, Arms factories, and Siege Artillery sections—dark-green caps with visors and chin straps; black band with red piping around both edges and cut-out numerals or letters backed by yellow cloth, as prescribed for combatants or craftsmen of these units; red piping around the top of the cap.

i.) Personnel holding a position as junior ordnance inspector (*unter-tseikhvarter*) within the Artillery administration—dark-green caps without visors; black band with red piping around both edges and the cut-out letter A. backed by yellow cloth; red piping around the top of the cap [283].

24 November 1847 - Unattached officers of the **Garrison Artillery branch** (*chislyashchies' po Garnizonnoi Artillerii*) are prescribed the uniform clothing of Garrison Artillery brigades, with the only differences being that instead of helmet and half-saber, they wear hats and rapiers and have epaulettes with a silver field, while buttons are without any Garrison brigade number (Illus. 578) [284].

24 November 1848 and 25 November 1849 - The Garrison Artillery in the **Separate Caucasus Corps** is prescribed the uniforms and equipment of 8 August, 23 September, 31 October, and 24 November 1848, and 25 November 1849, as described above in detail for Grenadier regiments (Illus. 579) [285].

1 September 1849 - Unattached field and company-grade officers of the **Garrison Artillery branch** are ordered to wear, instead of hats, helmets with the badge established for the Garrison Artillery, i.e. with silver mountings, no plume, and without any number on the grenade (Illus. 580) [286].

9 and 25 November 1849 - The manner of fitting the **helmet** is confirmed, as laid out in detail above for Grenadier regiments [287].

15 February 1850 - Officers are prescribed the same uniform and armament as were ordered for the forces of the **Separate**

Caucasus Corps on 8 August 1848, and as described in detail above for Grenadier regiments, but with the appropriate differences in colors and trim, and also the following modifications:

    a.) The top of the **headdress** has silver galloon that has a wide red stripe edged in black down the center, and along the edges of the galloon two narrow red stripes.

    b.) On the **half-caftan** the collar is as it was on the former coat; cuffs of black cloth; red piping down the front and along the skirts, along the upper edge of the cuffs, and on the pocket flaps.

    c.) *Sharavary* **pants** of dark-green cloth with the same piping as on the previous pants [288].

8 July 1851 - Approval is given to the **drum, water flask, greatcoat strap,** and **sword belt** as described and laid out in detail under this date for Grenadier regiments [289].

10 January 1852 - In district and local Arsenals, local Artillery parks, Powder works, Arms factories, and Cartridge establishments (*Kapsyul'nyya zavedeniya*), **knapsacks** with straps, **water flasks,** and **greatcoat cases** are withdrawn for lower ranks [290].

14 July 1853 - For the Garrison Artillery Brigade of the **Siberia District,** which is prescribed the uniform of Field Artillery, helmet plates and buttons are ordered to be without numbers, but with the artillery insignia [291].

8 May 1854 - Lower ranks of the Combined Battery of the **Finland District's** Artillery Garrisons are ordered to have the Cyrillic letters S.B. ("*Svodnaya Batareya*") on their forage caps, without any number [292].

28 - GARRISON ENGINEERS (*GARNIZONNYE INZHENERY*).

11 February 1826 - Garrison Engineer officers, instead of dark-green pants with high boots and grey riding trousers with wide stripes, are given long dark-green **pants** with red piping on the side seams (Illus. 581) [293].

26 July 1826 - Garrison Engineer officers, during the summer, when officers in troop units are in summer pants with gaiters, are ordered to likewise wear **summer pants,** of the pattern established on 11 February for dark-green pants (Illus. 582) [294].

18 August 1826 - These officers, when performing inspections on work outside the capitals, are ordered to be in **half-uniform** (*poluforma*), i.e. in frock coat (*syurtuk*) with epaulettes, without a sword, and wearing the forage cap [295].

1 January 1827 - Garrison Engineer officers' **epaulettes** are to have small forged and stamped gold stars as rank distinctions, of the same pattern and scheme as for the other infantry troops described above [296].

16 December 1829 - Garrison Engineer officers are to have the cuffs on their **frock coats** (*syurtuki*) are changed from black to dark green as previously, with red piping [297].

26 December 1829 - Garrison Engineer officers are directed to have the **buttons** on their coats, frock coats, and greatcoats made with the raised image of a small single-flame grenade [298].

8 June 1832 - Officers are permitted to wear **moustaches** [299].

15 July 1837 - A new pattern of officers' **sash** is approved, identical to that introduced at this time for other branches and described above [300].

17 December 1837 - A new pattern of officers' **epaulette** is approved, identical with that introduced at this time for other branches, i.e. with the additon of a fourth twist of braid [301].

4 January 1839 - Officers' **pants** and **trousers** are not to have any bows or bands on the front, but are to be completely plain in the manner prescribed for lower ranks [302].

23 January 1841 - The capes of officers' **greatcoats** are to be 28 inches long as measured from the lower edge of the collar [303].

2 January 1844 - Officers are to have a **cockade** on the cap band of the forage cap [304].

2 February 1846 - Garrison Engineer officers are given **helmets** in place of hats, without plumes and with a badge of two crossed axes below a three-flame grenade (Illus 583) [305].

13 October 1849 - Instead of rapiers (*shpagi*), officers are ordered to carry **half-sabers** (*polusabli*) (Illus. 584) [306].

15 February 1850 - Field and company-grade officers are prescribed the same uniform and armament as were ordered for the forces of the **Separate Caucasus Corps** on 8 August 1848, and as described in detail above for Grenadier regiments, but with the appropriate differences in colors and trim, and also the following modifications:

    a.) The top of the **headdress** has silver galloon that has a wide black stripe down the center, and along the edges of the galloon two narrow red stripes.

    b.) On the **half-caftan** the collar is as it was on the former coat; cuffs without flaps, of black cloth; red cloth piping down the front to the bottom of the skirts, along the upper edge of the cuffs, and on the pocket flaps.

    c.) *Sharavary* **pants** of dark-green cloth with the same piping as on the previous pants (Illus. 585) [307].

29 - MILITARY-LABOR COMPANIES OF THE ENGINEER ADMINISTRATION AND MARINE CONSTRUCTION SECTION (*VOENNO-RABOCHIYA ROTY INZHENERNAGO VEDOMSTVA I MORSKOI STROITEL'NOI CHASTI*).

11 February 1826 - Officers of Military-Labor companies of the Engineer administration, in place of their previous dark-green pants with high boots, and lower ranks, in place of their pants with knee gaiters (*kragi*), are given dark-green **pants** with red piping on the side seams. Lower ranks at all times, and company-grade officers only when in formation with sashes, are ordered to wear black cloth **half-gaiters** (*polushtiblety*) under these pants and over the boots, fastened with five or six small white buttons. Along with this change, the horizontal belt for the **knapsack** is to be between the two lower buttons on the front of the coat, while the **greatcoat** is carried on the knapsack rolled into a tube in its special oilskin case made of raven's-duck (*ravenduchnaya kleenka*). (Illus. 586) [308].

15 September 1826 - Lower ranks who have served out the regulation number of years yet voluntarily remain in service are ordered to wear a **gold galloon chevron** (*nashivka iz zolotnago galuna*) on the left sleeve, as related above for Garrison Artillery [309].

1 January 1827 - Officers' epaulettes, in addition to any existing number on them, are to have little gold forged or stamped **stars** (*kovannyya zvezdochki*) as rank distinctions, of the same form and according to the same scheme as described above for other infantry troops [310].

14 December 1827 - The **chevrons** established on 15 September 1826 for the left sleeves of lower ranks are ordered to be silver instead of gold, [311].

24 March 1828 - Lower ranks' **coats** are not to be tailored with cinches (*peretyazhki*) [312].

13 April 1828 - The newly established **Military-Labor companies of the Marine Construction Section** are prescribed the same uniforms and armament as Military-Labor companies of the Engineer Administration, with only the addition of white piping on the dress coat's cuff flaps (Illus. 587) [313].

24 April 1828 - Military-Labor companies are given a new model **shako** (*kiver*), identical to that introduced at this time for other infantry troops, except without cords for lower ranks. The shako badge remains as before, i.e. two crossed spades (Illus. 587 and 588). Along with the new shako pattern there are the following changes:

1.) The **sword-belt** (*portupeya*) is prescribed to be 2 vershoks (3 1/2 inches) wide; the **shoulder belts for the knapsack** (*rantsevye plechevye remni*) — 1 1/2 vershoks (2 5/8 inches); and the **belt across the chest** (*nagrudnyi remen*) — 1 1/8 vershoks (2 inches).

2.) The knapsack is prescribed to be 9 vershoks (15 3/4 inches) broad, 8 vershoks (14 inches) high, and 2 vershoks (4 3/8 inches) wide. The length of the cover from the upper edge is 6 vershoks (10 1/2 inches).

3.) In place of their grey coats (*mundiry*), all **non-combatant non-commissioned officers** are issued with dark-green **frock coats** (*syurtuki*) with a single row of buttons and the same collar, cuffs, and shoulder straps as for combatant personnel. **Pants**, however, are grey with red piping on the side seams [314].

10 August 1829 - Military-Labor companies in the Georgia Engineer District (*Gruzinskii Inzhenernyi Okrug*) are ordered have black **sheepskin headdresses** (*ovchinnyya shapki*) in place of the shako, identical to those introduced at this time for other infantry troops in the Separate Caucasus Corps, but without pompons and with the same badge as was on the shakos (Illus. 589) [315].

29 November 1829 - Conductors are ordered to have the same **sword knots** as in Sapper and Pioneer battalions (Illus. 477) [13].

16 December 1829 - The black **cuffs** of officers' frock coats in Military-Labor companies of the Engineer Administration are changed to dark green as before (the same color as the frock coat), with red piping [316].

26 December 1829 - Officers and lower ranks of Military-Labor companies are directed to have their **buttons** made with the raised image two crossed spades and above them the company number [317].

8 June 1832 - Officers are permitted to wear **moustaches** [318].

3 January 1833 - Cloth **half-gaiters** (*polushtiblety*) are abolished for company-grade officers and lower ranks [319].

20 February 1833 - In Military-Labor companies the summer pants with buttons and integral spats (*kozyrki*) are replaced by **breeches** without buttons or spats (Illus. 590) [320].

22 February 1833 - Field and company-grade officers are ordered not to use the hat, but rather wear the **shako** at all times [321].

29 January 1834 - In order to introduce uniformity to shako **chin straps**, it is ordered that they be of black Russian leather, 1/2 vershok (7/8 inch) wide, sewn to the left side of the shako underneath the lower reinforcement strap, flush, and fastened by a button sewn onto the right side of the shako above the lower reinforcement [322].

26 September 1834 - Lower ranks are directed to wear the **knapsack** on two belts lying crosswise over the chest [323].

18 April 1835 - Officers are ordered to carry, instead of a rapier (*shpaga*), the **half-sabers** (*polusabli*) prescribed for infantry officers [324].

20 August 1835 - It is ordered that:

1) Officers wear the **knapsack** using only two shoulder belts, without any cross strap or chest strap. These belts are to be lacquered.

2) For lower ranks a **linen case** (*kholshchevyi chekhol*) or pocket (*karman*) for the forage cap is to be put on the outside of the knapsack on the side that lies on the soldier's back. These cases are to be made from the linings of wornout coats.

3) For drummers the **knapsack** is to have one belt as before, worn over the left shoulder [325].

18 December 1835 - **Buttons** are ordered to be smooth in all Military-Labor companies of the Engineer Administration and Marine Construction Section [326].

31 January 1836 - Lower ranks' **greatcoats** (*shineli*) are to have nine buttons instead of ten: six along the front opening, two on the shoulder straps, and one on the flap behind [327].

27 April 1836 - **Pompons** are to be lined with black leather [328].

15 July 1837 - A new pattern of officers' **sash** (*sharf*) is confirmed, identical to that introduced at this time for other branches [329].

17 December 1837 - A new pattern for officers' **epaulettes** is confirmed, identical to that introduced at this time for other branches and described above [330].

4 January 1839 - Field and company-grade officers are not to have any bows or bands (*banty*) on the front of their **pants** or **trousers**. These are to be worn completely smooth in the manner prescribed for lower ranks [331].

16 March 1839 - Lower ranks' **sword-belts** (*portupei*) are to be 1 1/2 vershoks (2 5/8 inches) wide, while drummers' are 2 1/2 vershoks (4 2/5 inches), as before [332].

16 October 1840 - Lower ranks who voluntarily remain in service after completing the regulation period for retirement are to be given for subsequent service a sewn-on **chevron of silver galloon** to be worn on the left sleeve, one every five years that are served [333].

23 January 1841 - The capes (*bolshie vorotniki*) of officers' **greatcoats** are to be 1 arshin (28 inches) long as measured from the lower edge of the collar (*malyi vorotnik*) [334].

26 November 1842 - Until a new uniform is approved, Military-Labor companies in the Georgia Engineer District are to wear **forage caps** in place of the sheepskin headdress [335].

16 January 1843 - To distinguish lower ranks who have committed transgressions and undergone punishments, thin grey and black **sewn-on cords** (*nashivki iz tonkago snurka*) are established, on the same basis as related above for Line battalions [336].

21 February 1843 - The aforementioned grey and black **cords** are ordered to be sewn onto the shoulder straps of greatcoats as well as dress coats, below the cut-out number [337].

8 April 1843 - Officers and lower ranks of Military-Labor companies (except in the Georgia District) with **shakos** are ordered to have these according to a new pattern: 4 3/4 vershoks (8 1/3 inches) high and curving slightly inward toward the bottom (Illus. 592). Along with this, trim on the shoulder straps (*nashivki na plechevye pogony*) of sergeants (*feldfebeli*), non-commissioned officers (*unter-ofitsery*), and lance-corporals (*yefreitory*) is established following the same scheme as for these ranks in infantry regiments [338].

2 January 1844 - Officers are to have a **cockade** (*kokarda*) on the band of their forage caps, identical to that introduced at this time for other branches [339].

8 May 1844 - In Military-Labor companies (except in the Georgia District), shakos (*kivera*) are replaced by **helmets** (*kaski*), of the same pattern as established at this time for other infantry troops, without a plume, and with the same badge as was on the shako (Illus. 593 and 594) [340].

20 May 1844 - With the general allocation of **forage-cap** particulars throughout the Army, lower ranks of Military-Labor companies keep their caps as before—dark green with a black cloth band piped red along the edges, the same piping around the crown, and with cut-out company numerals and a Cyrillic letter, backed by yellow cloth: for Military-Labor Company Nº 1—1.R., for Company Nº 2—2.R., etc. Officers have the same forage caps but without numbers or letters and with a visor [341].

4 January 1845 - Officers' **helmets** are to have, on the right side under the chin-scales, a cockade, of the pattern used on hats (Illus. 595) [342].

15 February 1850 - Field and company-grade officers of Military-Labor companies of the Engineer Administration (in the Georgia District - M.C.), are prescribed the same uniforms and armament as ordered for troops of the **Separate Caucasus Corps** on 8 August 1848, but with the appropriate differences in colors and trim and also the following alterations:

a.) The top of the **headdress** has silver galloon with a wide black stripe down the center, and two narrow red stripes along the edges of the galloon.

b.) On the **half-caftan** the collar is as it was on the dress coat; cuffs are without flaps, of black cloth; red cloth piping around the collar, down the front to the bottom of the skirts, around the upper edge of the cuffs, and on the pocket flaps.

c.) *Sharavary* **pants** of dark-green cloth with red piping [343].

30 - ARSENAL COMPANIES OF THE ENGINEER ADMINISTRATION (*ARSENAL'NYYA ROTY INZHENERNAGO VEDOMSTVA*).

9 February 1832 - With the establishment of **Arsenal companies**, they are prescribed the same uniforms and armaments as Military-Labor companies, with differences only in the epaulettes, shoulder straps, and bands of lower ranks' forage caps, these being ordered to have: in Arsenal Company N° 1— the numeral and letter *1.A.*, and in Arsenal Company N° 2— the numeral and letter *2.A.* [344]. Also, on shakos the spades are replaced by axes (Illus. 596) [345].

13 March 1832 - With the disbanding of Company N° 2, **Company N° 1** is ordered not to have any number, and consequently only the letter *A.* remains on epaulettes, shoulder straps, and forage caps [346]. However, the changes that occured since 1832 in Military-Labor companies of the Engineer Administration were extended in equal force to Arsenal companies.

19 May 1847 - With the new general allocation of **forage-cap** colors throughout the Army, clerks, medics, and other lower ranks in Arsenal companies of the Engineer Administration are prescribed dark-green forage caps with a black band piped on both edges with red, and with the cut-out Cyrillic letters *A.R.* backed with yellow cloth. Piping around the crown—red [347].

21 July 1849 - **Officers of Arsenal companies** of the Engineer Administration are ordered to have the standard sapper dress coat and, in place of hats and rapiers, helmets and half-sabers. The plate on the helmet is to be of the sapper pattern, with two crossed axes, and on buttons and helmet plates—the Cyrillic letters *I.A.* [348].

31 - PARK HALF-COMPANIES OF THE ENGINEER ADMINISTRATION (*PARKOVYYA POLUROTY INZHENERNAGO VEDOMSTVA*).

13 March 1842 - With the establishment of **Park half-companies**, they are prescribed the same uniforms and armaments as Military-Labor and Arsenal companies, with differences only in officer' epaulettes and lower ranks' shoulder straps and forage caps, which in Half-Company N° 1 are ordered to have the numeral and Cyrillic letter *1.P.*, and in Half-Company N° 2— the numeral and Cyrillic letter *2.P.* [349].

19 May 1847 - Clerks, medics, and other lower ranks in Park half-companies of the Engineer Administration are prescribed dark-green **forage caps** with a black band piped on both edges with red, and with the cut-out N° of the half-company and the Cyrillic letter *P.*, backed with yellow cloth; red piping around the crown [350].

21 July 1849 - **Officers of Park half-companies** are ordered to have the standard sapper dress coat, helmets, and half-sabers. The plate on the helmet is to be of the sapper pattern, with two crossed axes, and on buttons and helmet plates—the same numerals and letters as on the epaulettes [351].

32 - MILITARY-LABOR BATTALIONS AND COMPANIES OF THE MILITARY SETTLEMENTS ADMINISTRATION (*VOENNO-RABOCHIYA BATALIONY I ROTY VEDOMSTVA VOENNYKH POSELENII*).

11 February 1826 - Field and company-grade officers and lower combatant ranks of Military-Labor companies, in place of their previous dark-green pants with high boots, and lower ranks, in place of their similar pants with knee gaiters (*kragi*), are given dark-green **pants** with light-green piping on the side seams (Illus. 597). Lower ranks at all times, and company-grade officers only when in formation with sashes, are ordered to wear black cloth **half-gaiters** (*polushtiblety*) under these pants and over the boots, fastened with five or six small white buttons. Along with this change, the horizontal belt for the **knapsack** is ordered to be between the two lower buttons on the front of the coat [352].

24 April 1828 - Officers and lower ranks are given a new **shako** (*kiver*), identical to that intruduced at this time for Military-Labor companies of the Engineer Administration (Illus. 598) [353].

17 August 1829 - The **4th Company of Military-Labor Battalion N° 1** (at the Caucasus Mineral Waters), for defense against bandit raids, are ordered to have muskets and retain their short swords (*tesaki*), which at this time are withdrawn from the other three companies of the battalion and all companies of Battalion N° 2 [354].

26 December 1829 - Officers and lower ranks of Military-Labor Battalions are directed to have their **buttons** made with the raised image two crossed spades and above them the company number [355].

28 January 1832 - The newly established **Military-Labor battalion in the Separate Caucasus Corps** is ordered to have the same uniforms, armaments, and accouterments as other Military-Labor battalions, except that instead of shakos it is to be given forage caps of dark-green cloth with a black band, with light-green piping and a black chin strap fastening to a tin button sewn onto the band, and on buttons there are crossed shapes without a number (Illus. 599) [599].

7 August 1832 - In the **Moscow Military-Labor Company** (*Moskovskaya Voenno-rabochaya rota*), which has the same uniform as Military-Labor battalions, buttons are ordered to be smooth and shoulder straps have the Cyrillic letters *M.V.R.* [357].

8 April 1843 - Officers and lower ranks of Military-Labor battalions and Military-Labor companies of the Military Settlements Administration are given a new pattern **shako** that curves slightly inward toward the bottom, like those established at this time for other troops [358].

2 January 1844 - Officers are to have a **cockade** (*kokarda*) on the band of their forage caps, identical to that introduced at this time for other branches [359].

9 May 1844 - In Military-Labor battalions and Military-Labor companies of the Military Settlements Administration, shakos (*kivera*) are replaced by **helmets** (*kaski*), of the same pattern established at this time for Military-Labor companies of the Engineer Administration and with the same badge (Illus. 600) [360].

4 January 1845 - Officers' **helmets** are ordered to have a cockade as established at this time for officers' helmets in other branches (Illus. 601) [361].

In addition to the changes shown here, orders regarding Military-Labor companies of the Engineer Administration were extended in equal measure to Military-Labor battalions and Military-Labor companies of the Military Settlements Administration: **15 September 1826**—on gold sewn-on chevrons; **1 January 1827**—on small stars for epaulettes; **14 December 1827**—on silver sewn-on chevrons; **24 March 1828**—on not allowing cinches; **24 April 1828**—on reducing the width of sword belts and knapsack straps, on changes in the knapsacks, and regarding uniforms for noncombatants; **16 December 1829**—on cuffs on officers' frock coats; **8 June 1832**—on wearing moustaches; **3 January 1833**—on abolishing gaiters on winter pants; **20 February 1833**—on changing summer pants; **22 February 1833**—on officers not wearing the sash; **26 September 1834**—on the introduction of crossed belts for the knapsack; **20 August 1835**—on knapsacks for officers and lower ranks; **31 January 1836**—on greatcoat buttons; **27 April 1836**—on shako pompons; **15 July 1837**—on new-pattern officers' sashes; **17 December 1837**—on changing the pattern of officers' epaulettes; **4 January 1839**—on officers' pants and breeches; **16 March 1839**—on lower ranks' accouterments; **16 October 1840**—on sewn-on chevrons; **23 January 1841**—on officers' greatcoats; **16 January** and **21 February 1843**—on distinguishing lower ranks who have undergone punishments; and **8 April 1843**—regarding trim on shoulder straps.

19 May 1847 - Military-Labor battalions and companies of the Military Settlements Administration are ordered to have dark-green **forage caps** with a black band piped on both edges in light green, and with the cut-out company number and the Cyrillic letter *R.*, backed by light-green cloth; light-green piping around the crown of the cap [362].

19 June 1847 - The **temporary labor company** (*vremennaya rabochaya rota*) established on this date in the Novgorod District's 5th Agricultural Soldiers' Region is prescribed the same uniform as temporary labor companies in Cavalry Regions of the New-Russia Military Settlements [363].

13 October 1849 - Officers are ordered to carry infantry **half-sabers** instead of rapiers (Illus. 602) [364].

33 - PENAL COMPANIES OF THE ENGINEER ADMINISTRATION (*ARESTANTSKIYA ROTY INZHENERNAGO VEDOMSTVA*).

a.) For officers and lower ranks:

9 February 1827 - Since the time Penal companies of the Engineer Administration were given numbers, **officers and lower ranks** of these companies had in all regards the same uniforms and armaments as officers and lower ranks of the

Military-Labor companies of the same administration, except with axes on the shako instead of spades, with black lining on epaulettes and small cross straps instead of red, and with the company number and the letter *A.* on epaulettes and shoulder straps, viz.: *1 A., 2.A.I*, etc. (Illus. 603). When with prisoners performing labor duties, officers as well as non-commissioned officers are prescribed canes (*trosti*) [365].

Furthermore, on 14 August 1834, lower ranks in Penal companies were ordered to not have any special work clothing (*rabochaya odezhda*) except short fur or fleece coats (*polushubki*) and mittens with liners (*rukavitsy s varegami*) [366].

b.) For convicts (*arestanty*):

Since 1830 convicts were prescribed two kinds of clothing: winter—of peasant cloth, and summer—of raven's duck, with the following differences according to grade:

1.) *Convicts of the 1st grade* (with definite sentences) (*1-go razryada* (*srochnye*)), *winter clothing*—grey jacket (*kurtka*) with two rows of buttons covered in the same, with black sleeves and cuffs and black quadrangles (*chetyrekhugol'niki*) on the back; grey pants (Illus. 604). (*Note: in the plates, the "quadrangles" are shown mostly as a diamond shape but also as a square - M.C.*)

2.) *Convicts of the same grade, summer clothing*—white jacket with two rows of buttons covered in the same, with black cuffs and a black quadrangle on the back; white pants. For summer as well as winter dress a forage cap of grey cloth was prescribed, with two black stripes sewn crosswise on the upper crown and then continuing to the lower edge of the cap band (Illus. 604).

3.) *Convicts of the 2nd grade* (vagrants (*brodyagi*)), *winter clothing*—grey jacket with a black quadrangle on the back; grey pants (Illus. 605).

4.) *Convicts of the same grade, summer clothing*—white jacket with black quadrangle on the back; white pants. Grey forage cap with four black rectangles on the sides between the cap band and top of the crown (Illus. 605).

5.) *Convicts of the 3rd grade* (with life sentences (*vsegdashnie*))—winter jacket and winter pants of the pattern for the preceding but the entire right side grey and the left side black (Illus. 606).

6.) *Convicts of the same grade, summer clothing*—white jacket with black flaps sewn onto the cuffs, and with a black circle on the back; white pants. The right half of the forage cap grey, the left black (Illus. 606).

Besides these distinctions, convicts of the 1st and 2nd grades have the front half of their heads shaved from one ear to the other, while convicts of the 3rd grade have the left side of their heads shaved from the back of the neck to the forehead. Convicts of all three grades are prescribed black neckcloths [367].

15 February 1850 - Officers of Penal companies in the Caucasus are prescribed the same uniforms and armament as troops of the **Separate Caucaus Corps** were ordered to have on 8 August 1848, but with the appropriate differences in colors and trim and the following modifications:

a) The top of the **headdress** has silver galloon with a wide black stripe down the center, and two narrow red stripes along the edges of the galloon.

b.) On the **half-caftan** the collar is as it was on the dress coat; cuffs are without flaps, of black cloth; red cloth piping around the collar, down the front to the bottom of the skirts, around the upper edge of the cuffs, and on the pocket flaps.

c.) *Sharavary* **pants** of dark-green cloth with the piping that was on the previous pants [368].

10 January 1852 - Knapsacks with their straps, **water flasks**, and **greatcoat cases** with straps are all withdrawn from lower ranks [369].

NOTES

(196) Collection of Laws and Directives, 1826, Book I, pgs. 105 and 125.

(197) Ibid., Book II, pg. 76.

(198) Ibid., Book III, pg. 255.

(199) Ibid., 1827, Book I, pg. 3.

(200) Ibid., 1828, Book I, pg. 211.

(201) Ibid., Book II, pg. 131 et seq.

(202) Ibid., 1829, Book, III, pg. 129.

(203) Ibid., Book IV, pg. 3.

(204) Ibid., 1830, Book III, pg. 179.

(205) Ibid., 1832, Book II, pg. 545.

(206) Ibid., 1833, Book I, pg. 419.

(207) Ibid., pg. 435.

(208) Ibid., pg. 463.

(209) Ibid., pg. 465.

(210) Ibid., 1834, Book I, pg. 197.

(211) Ibid., Book III, pg. 465.

(212) Ibid., 1835, Book III, pg. 179.

(213) Ibid., 1836, Book I, pg. 137.

(214) Ibid., Book II, pg. 171.

(215) Ibid., 1837, Book III, pg. 47.

(216) Ibid., Book IV, pg. 325.

(217) Ibid., 1839, Book I, pg. 3.

(218) Ibid., pg. 179.

(219) Order of the Minister of War, 16 October 1840, N° 71.

(220) Ibid., 23 January 1841, N° 8.

(221) Ibid., 19 March 1841, N° 23.

(222) Archive of the Inspection Department of the War Ministry, correspondence for 1842, Sect. 2, 2nd Desk, N° 365.

(223) Order of the Minister of War, 8 April 1843, N°N° 46 and 47.

(224) Ibid., 10 May 1843, N° 63.

(225) Ibid., 2 January 1844, N° 1.

(226) Ibid., 9 May 1844, N° 1.

(227) Ibid., 4 January 1845, N° 1.

(228) Ibid., 8 March 1847, N° 46.

(229) Ibid., 8 August 1848, N° 148.

(230) Orders of the Minister of War, 9 and 25 November 1849, N°N° 110 and 117.

(231) Order of the Minister of War, 17 January 1851, N° 7.

(232) Ibid., 13 December 1851, N° 134.

(233) Archive of the Inspection Department of the War Ministry, correspondence of Sect. 2, 3rd Desk, N° 163, part 4, sheets 20, 129, 81, and 140.

(234) Information from the Commissariat Department of the War Ministry.

(235) Description of uniforms and weapons for officers of the IMPERIAL Russian Army, St. Petersburg, 1845, Book III, pgs. 281 and 282, and information from the Commissariat Department of the War Ministry.

(236) Collection of Laws and Directives, 1838, Book II, pg. 217.

(237) Order of the Minister of War, 9 May 1844, N° 63.

(238) Information from the Commissariat Department of the War Ministry.

(239) Information from the same Department.

(240) Collection of Laws and Directives, 1829, Book IV, pg. 3.

(241) Order of the Minister of War, 30 June 1853, N° 45.

(242) Collection of Laws and Directives, 1826, Book I, pg. 105.

(243) Ibid., Book II, pg. 76.

(244) Ibid., Book III, pg. 303.

(245) Information from the Commissariat Department of the War Ministry.

(246) Collection of Laws and Directives, 1826, Book III, pg. 255.

(247) Ibid., 1827, Book I, pg. 3.

(248) Ibid., Book IV, pg. 257.

(249) Ibid., 1828, Book I, pg. 211.

(250) Information from the Commissariat Department of the War Ministry.

(251) Collection of Laws and Directives, 1829, Book III, pg. 129, and information from the Commissariat Department of the War Ministry.

(252) Collection of Laws and Directives, 1829, Book VI, pg. 107.

(253) Ibid., 1830, Book I, pg. 103.

(254) Ibid., 1832, Book II, pg. 545.

(255) Ibid., Book IV, pg. 125.

(256) Ibid., 1833, Book I, pg. 419.

(257) Ibid., pg. 463.

(258) Ibid., pg. 465.

(259) Ibid., Book III, pg. 207.

(260) Ibid., Book IV, pg. 53.

(261) Ibid., 1834, Book I, pg. 193.

(262) Ibid., pg. 197.

(263) Ibid., Book III, pg. 465.

(264) Ibid., 1835, Book III, pg. 179.

(265) Ibid., 1836, Book I, pg. 137.

(266) Ibid., Book II, pg. 171.

(267) Ibid., 1837, Book III, pg. 47.

(268) Ibid., Book IV, pg. 325.

(269) Ibid., 1839, Book I, pg. 3.

(270) Ibid., pg. 179.

(271) Order of the Minister of War, 16 October 1840, N° 71.

(272) Ibid., 23 January 1841, N° 8.

(273) Archive of the Inspection Department of the War Ministry, correspondence for 1842, Sect. 2, 2nd Desk, N° 365.

(274) Order of the Minister of War, 16 January 1843, N° 6.

(275) Ibid., 21 February 1843, N° 24.

(276) Ibid., 8 April 1843, N°N° 46 and 47.

(277) Ibid., 2 January 1844, N° 1.

(278) Ibid., 9 May 1844, N° 63.

(279) Ibid., 20 May 1844, N° 69.

(280) Ibid., 4 January 1845, N° 1.

(281) Ibid., 6 February 1846, N° 33.

(282) Correspondence of the Minister of War with His Highness's Chief of Staff for the Master-General of Ordance [*General-Fel'dtseikhmeister*], 4 November 1846, N° 10112.

(283) Order of the Minister of War, 19 May 1847, N° 86.

(284) Correspondence of the Minister of War with His Highness's Chief of Staff for the Master-General of Ordance [*General-Fel'dtseikhmeister*], 24 November 1847, N° 10638.

(285) Orders of the Minister of War, 24 November 1848, N° 179, and 25 November 1849, N° 118.

(286) Order of the Minister of War, 1 September 1849, N° 84.

(287) Orders of the Minister of War, 9 and 25 November 1849, N°N° 110 and 117.

(288) Order of the Minister of War, 15 February 1850, N° 13.

(289) Ibid., 13 December 1851, N° 134.

(290) Ibid., 10 January 1852, N° 4, § 45.

(291) Ibid., 14 July 1853, N° 53.

(292) HIGHEST order to the Inspector of All Artillery, 8 May 1854, N° 5232.

(293) Collection of Laws and Directives, 1826, Book I, pg. 105.

(294) Ibid., Book III, pg. 161.

(295) Ibid., pg. 197.

(296) Ibid., 1827, Book I, pg. 3.

(297) Ibid., 1829, Book IV, pg. 107.

(298) Ibid., pg. 118.

(299) Ibid., 1832, Book II, pg. 545.

(300) Ibid., 1837, Book III, pg. 47.

(301) Ibid., Book IV, pg. 325.

(302) Ibid., 1839, Book I, pg. 3.

(303) Order of the Minister of War, 23 January 1841, N° 8.

(304) Ibid., 2 January 1844, N° 1.

(305) Ibid., 2 February 1846, N° 26.

(306) Ibid., 13 October 1849, N° 104.

(307) Ibid., 15 February 1850, N° 13.

(308) Collection of Laws and Directives, 1826, Book I, pg. 105.

(309) Ibid., Book III, pg. 255.

(310) Ibid., 1827, Book I, pg. 3.

(311) Ibid., Book IV, pg. 257.

(312) Ibid., 1828, Book I, pg. 211.

(313) Ibid., Book II, pg. 55, § 6.

(314) Ibid., pgs. 131 et seq.

(315) Ibid., 1829, Book III, pg. 129.

(316) Ibid., Book IV, pg. 107.

(317) Ibid., pg. 118.

(318) Ibid., 1832, Book II, pg. 545.

(319) Ibid., 1833, Book I, pg. 419.

(320) Ibid., pg. 463.

(321) Ibid., pg. 465.

(322) Ibid., 1834, Book I, pg. 197.

(323) Ibid., Book III, pg. 465.

(324) Ibid., 1835, Book II, pg. 281.

(325) Ibid., Book III, pg. 10.

(326) Ibid., Book IV, pg. 197.

(327) Ibid., 1836, Book I, pg. 137.

(328) Ibid., Book II, pg. 171.

(329) Ibid., Book III, pg. 47.

(330) Collection of Laws and Directives, 1836, Book IV pg. 325.

(331) Ibid., 1839, Book I, N° 3.

(332) Ibid., pg. 179.

(333) Order of the Minister of War, 16 October 1840, N° 71.

(334) Ibid., 23 January 1841, N° 8.

(335) Archive of the Inspection Department of the War Ministry, correspondence for 1842, Sect. 2, 2nd Desk, N° 365.

(336) Order of the Minister of War, 16 January 1843, N° 6.

(337) Ibid., 21 February 1843, N° 24.

(338) Ibid., 8 April 1843, N°N° 46 and 47.

(339) Ibid., 2 January 1844, N° 1.
(340) Ibid., 9 May 1844, N° 63.
(341) Ibid., 20 May 1844, N° 69.
(342) Ibid., 4 January 1845, N° 1.
(343) Ibid., 15 February 1850, N° 13.
(344) Collection of Laws and Directives, 1832, Book I, pg. 91.
(345) Information from the Commissariat Department of the War Ministry.
(346) Order of the Minister of War, 13 March 1842, N° 22, § 7.
(347) Ibid., 19 March 1847, N° 86.
(348) Ibid., 21 July 1849, N° 66.
(349) Ibid., 13 March 1842, N° 22, § 7.
(350) Ibid., 19 March 1847, N° 86.
(351) Ibid., 21 July 1849, N° 66.
(352) Collection of Laws and Directives, 1826, Book I, pg. 105.
(353) Ibid., Book II, pg. 131 et seq.
(354) Ibid., 1830, Book I, pg. 109.
(355) Ibid., 1829, Book IV, pg. 118.
(356) Ibid., 1832, Book II, pg. 105 et seq.
(357) Ibid., Book III, pg. 395.
(358) Order of the Minister of War, 8 April 1843, N° 46 .
(359) Ibid., 2 January 1844, N° 1.
(360) Ibid., 9 May 1844, N° 63.
(361) Ibid., 4 January 1845, N° 1.
(362) Ibid., 19 May 1847, N° 86.
(363) Ibid., 19 July 1847, N° 105.
(364) Ibid., 13 October 1849, N° 104.
(365) Information from the Commissariat Department of the War Ministry.
(366) Collection of Laws and Directives, 1834, Book III, pg. 439.
(367) Information received from Penal companies.
(368) Order of the Minister of War, 15 February 1850, N° 13.
(369) Ibid., 10 January 1852, N° 4, § 45.

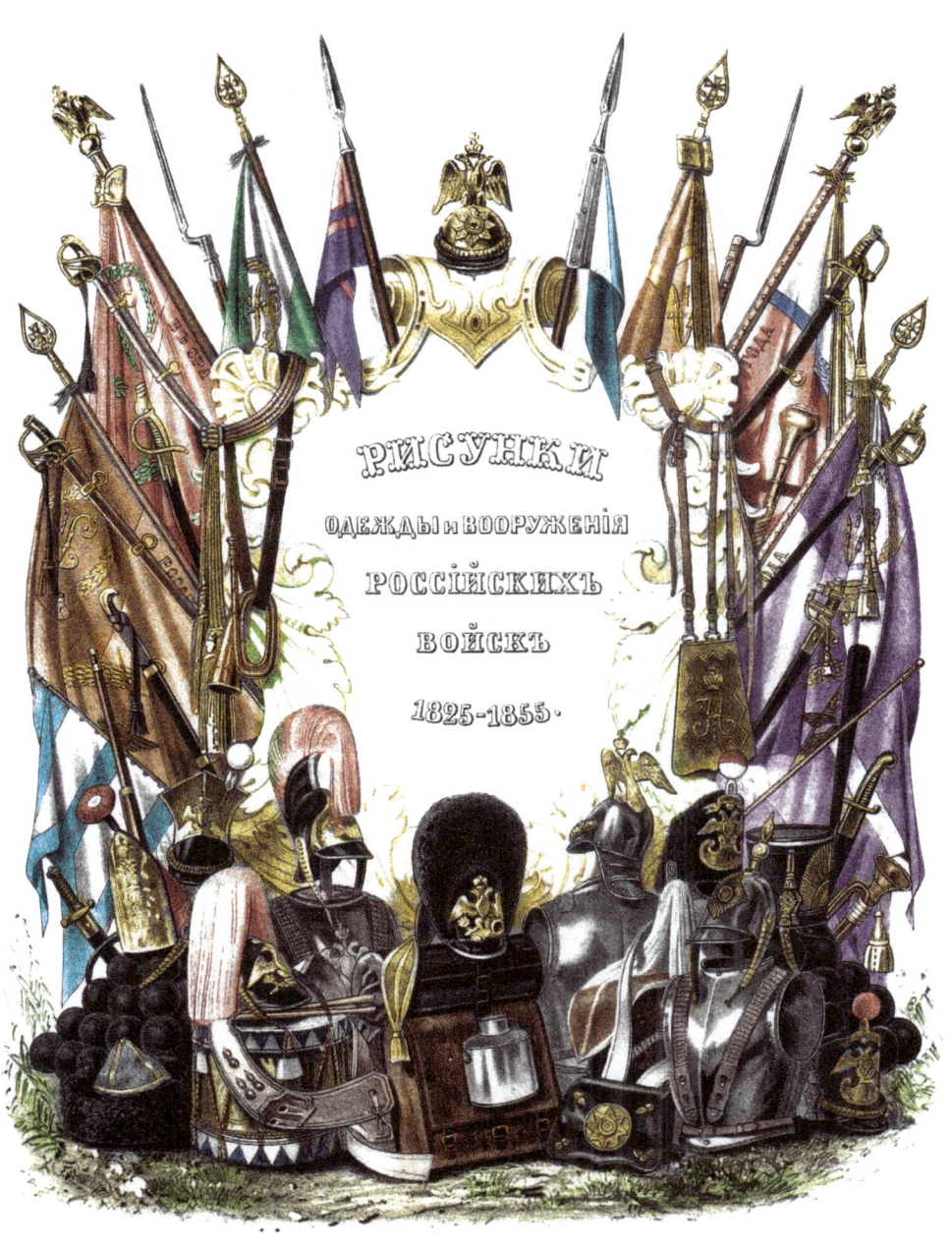

РИСУНКИ

ОДЕЖДЫ и ВООРУЖЕНІЯ

РОССІЙСКИХЪ

ВОЙСКЪ

1825-1855.

PLATES LIST OF ILLUSTRATIONS

580. Company-grade Officer. Garrison Artillery Branch. 1849-1855.

581. Company-grade Officer. Garrison Engineers. 1826-1846.

582. Company-grade Officer. Garrison Engineers. 1826-1846.

583. Company-grade Officer. Garrison Engineers. 1846-1849.

584. Company-grade Officer. Garrison Engineers. 1849-1855.

585. Company-grade Officer. Garrison Engineers in the Separate Caucasus Corps. 1850-1855.

586. Private and Company-grade Officer. Military-Labor Companies of the Engineer Administration. 1826-1828.

587. Non-commissioned Officer and Company-grade Officer. Military-Labor Companies of the Marine Construction Section. 1828-1835.

588. Company-grade Officer. Military-Labor Companies of the Engineer Administration. 1828-1833.

589. Drummer. Military-Labor Companies in the Georgia Engineer District. 1829-1833.

590. Private. Military-Labor Companies of the Marine Construction Section. 1833-1843.

591. Company-grade Officer. Military-Labor Companies of the Engineer Administration. 1835-1843.

592. Non-commissioned Officer, Private, and Drummer. Military-Labor Companies of the Engineer Administration. 1843 and 1844.

593. Company-grade Officers. Military-Labor Companies of the Engineer Administration and Marine Construction Section. 1844 and 1845.

594. Non-commissioned Officer. Military-Labor Companies of the Engineer Administration. 1844-1849.

595. Company-grade Officers. Military-Labor Companies of the Engineer Administration. 1845-1855.

596. Company-grade Officer. Arsenal Companies of the Engineer Administration. 1832 and 1833.

597. Company-grade Officer and Drummer. Military-Labor Battalions. 1826-1828.

598. Private. Military-Labor Battalions. 1828-1833.

599. Non-commissioned Officer. Caucasus Military-Labor Battalion. 1832 and 1833.

600. Private and Drummer. Military-Labor Battalions and Military-Labor Companies of the Military Settlements Administration. 1844-1849.

601. Company-grade Officer. Military-Labor Battalions and Military-Labor Companies of the Military Settlements Administration. 1845-1849.

602. Field-grade Officer. Military-Labor Battalions and Military-Labor Companies of the Military Settlements Administration. 1849-1855.

603. Non-commissioned Officer and Company-grade Officer. Penal Companies of the Engineer Administration. 1844-1849.

604. Convicts of the 1st Grade (Definite Sentences). Since 1830.

605. Convicts of the 2nd Grade (Vagrants). Since 1830.

606. Convicts of the 3rd Grade (Life Sentences). Since 1830.

Private. District Invalid Commands. 1826-1828.

Company-grade Officer. District Invalid Commands. 1826-1828.

Non-commissioned Officer. District Invalid Commands. 1826-1828.

Private. District Invalid Commands. 1828 and 1829.

Company-grade Officer. District Invalid Commands in the Separate Caucasus Corps. 1829.

Company-grade Officer and Private. District Invalid Commands. 1829-1833. (Note: in 1830 officers' rapiers were replaced by half-sabers.)

Private. District Invalid Commands. 1833-1843.

Company-grade Officer and Private. District Invalid Commands. 1844.

Private. District Invalid Commands in the Separate Caucasus Corps. 1848-1855.

Company-grade Officer. District Invalid Commands in the Separate Caucasus Corps. 1848-1855.

Private. Horse-Étape Commands. 1837-1844.

Company-grade Officer. Horse-Étape Commands. 1837-1844.

Company-grade Officer. Horse-Étape Commands. 1845-1849.

Private. Mobile Invalid Companies. 1826-1828.

Company-grade Officer. Mobile Invalid Companies. 1826-1828

Private. Mobile Invalid Companies. 1829-1855.

Cannoneer and Company-grade Officer. Garrison Artillery Companies. 1826-1828.

Fireworker. Garrison Artillery Companies. 1826-1828.

Fireworker. St.-Petersburg Arsenal. 1826-1828.

Master Craftsman. St.-Petersburg Arsenal. 1826-1855.

Fireworker. Laboratory Companies. 1826-1828.

Non-commissioned Officer. Okhtensk Powder Works. 1826-1828.

Private. Non-Settled Labor Companies of the Okhtensk Powder Works. 1826-1828.

Train Non-commissioned Officer and Soldier (Furshtatskii unter-ofitser i furleit). Okhtensk Powder Works. 1826-1855.

Company-grade Officer and Cannoneer. Garrison Artillery Companies. 1828-1833.

Fireworkers. St.-Petersburg Arsenal and Laboratory Companies. 1828-1833.

Company-grade Officer and Fireworker. Garrison Artillery Companies in the Caucasus and Georgia Districts. 1829-1833.

Officers' buttons for the Garrison Artillery, confirmed in March 1830.

Cannoneer. Garrison Artillery Companies. 1833-1843.

Company-grade Officer. Garrison Artillery Companies. 1833.

Company-grade Officer. Garrison Artillery Companies. 1833-1843.

Cannoneer. Garrison Artillery Companies. 1834-1343.

Company-grade Officer. Garrison Artillery Companies. Fireworker. St.-Petersburg Arsenal. 1843 and 1844.

Company-grade Officers. Garrison Artillery Companies. 1844-1855.

Company-grade Officer and Cannoneer. Garrison Artillery Companies. 1844 and 1845.

Field-grade Officer. St.-Petersburg Arsenal. Fireworker. Okhtensk Powder. Works. 1844 and 1845.

Company-grade Officer. Garrison Artillery Companies. 1845-1849.

Drummer. Garrison Artillery Companies. 1846-1849.

Field-grade Officer. Garrison Artillery Branch. 1847-1849.

Cannoneer. Garrison Artillery Companies in the Separate Caucasus Corps. 1848-1855.

Company-grade Officer. Garrison Artillery Branch. 1849-1855.

Company-grade Officer. Garrison Engineers. 1826-1846.

Company-grade Officer. Garrison Engineers. 1826-1846.

Company-grade Officer. Garrison Engineers. 1846-1849.

Company-grade Officer. Garrison Engineers. 1849-1855.

Company-grade Officer. Garrison Engineers in the Separate Caucasus Corps. 1850-1855.

Private and Company-grade Officer. Military-Labor Companies of the Engineer Administration. 1826-1828.

Non-commissioned Officer and Company-grade Officer. Military-Labor Companies of the Marine Construction Section. 1828-1835.

Company-grade Officer. Military-Labor Companies of the Engineer Administration. 1828-1833.

589

Drummer. Military-Labor Companies in the Georgia Engineer District. 1829-1833.

Private. Military-Labor Companies of the Marine Construction Section. 1833-1843.

Company-grade Officer. Military-Labor Companies of the Engineer Administration. 1835-1843.

Non-commissioned Officer, Private, and Drummer. Military-Labor Companies of the Engineer Administration. 1843 and 1844.

Company-grade Officers. Military-Labor Companies of the Engineer Administration and Marine Construction Section. 1844 and 1845.

Non-commissioned Officer. Military-Labor Companies of the Engineer Administration. 1844-1849.

Company-grade Officers. Military-Labor Companies of the Engineer Administration. 1845-1855.

Company-grade Officer. Arsenal Companies of the Engineer Administration. 1832 and 1833.

Company-grade Officer and Drummer. Military-Labor Battalions. 1826-1828.

Private. Military-Labor Battalions. 1828-1833.

Non-commissioned Officer. Caucasus Military-Labor Battalion. 1832 and 1833.

Private and Drummer. Military-Labor Batt and Military-Labor Companies of the Military Settlements Administration. 1844-1849.

Company-grade Officer. Military-Labor Batt. and Military-Labor Companies of the Military Settlements Administration. 1845-1849.

Field-grade Officer. Military-Labor Battalions and Military-Labor Companies of the Military Settlements Administration. 1849-1855.

3 POTA.

Non-commissioned Officer and Company-grade Officer. Penal Companies of the Engineer Administration. 1844-1849.

Convicts of the 1st Grade (Definite Sentences). Since 1830.

Convicts of the 2nd Grade (Vagrants). Since 1830.

Convicts of the 3rd Grade (Life Sentences). Since 1830.

SOLDIERS, WEAPONS & UNIFORMS ALREADY PUBLISHED
(SOME TITLES)

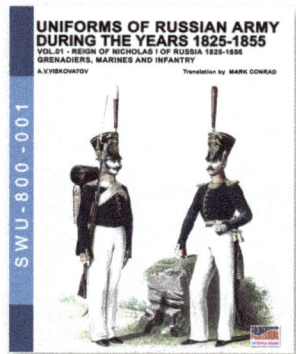

UNIFORMS OF RUSSIAN ARMY DURING THE YEARS 1825-1855
VOL.01 - REIGN OF NICHOLAS I OF RUSSIA 1825-1855
GRENADIERS, MARINES AND INFANTRY
A.V.VISKOVATOV — Translation by MARK CONRAD
SWU-800-001

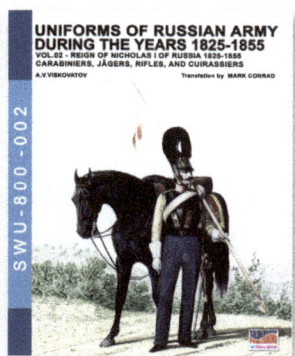

UNIFORMS OF RUSSIAN ARMY DURING THE YEARS 1825-1855
VOL.02 - REIGN OF NICHOLAS I OF RUSSIA 1825-1855
CARABINIERS, JÄGERS, RIFLES, AND CUIRASSIERS
A.V.VISKOVATOV — Translation by MARK CONRAD
SWU-800-002

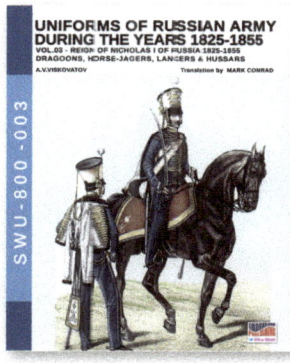

UNIFORMS OF RUSSIAN ARMY DURING THE YEARS 1825-1855
VOL.03 - REIGN OF NICHOLAS I OF RUSSIA 1825-1855
DRAGOONS, HORSE-JAGERS, LANCERS & HUSSARS
A.V.VISKOVATOV — Translation by MARK CONRAD
SWU-800-003

UNIFORMS OF RUSSIAN ARMY DURING THE YEARS 1825-1855
VOL.04 - REIGN OF NICHOLAS I OF RUSSIA 1825-1855
GENDARMES, TRAIN, ARTILLERY, SAPPERS & PIONEERS
A.V.VISKOVATOV — Translation by MARK CONRAD
SWU-800-004

UNIFORMS OF RUSSIAN ARMY DURING THE YEARS 1825-1855
VOL.05 - REIGN OF NICHOLAS I OF RUSSIA 1825-1855
ENGINEERS, GENERAL STAFF, GARRISON AND OTHERS
A.V.VISKOVATOV — Translation by MARK CONRAD
SWU-800-005

UNIFORMS OF RUSSIAN ARMY DURING THE YEARS 1825-1855
VOL.06 - REIGN OF NICHOLAS I OF RUSSIA 1825-1855
INVALID, GARRISON ARSENAL AND OTHERS
A.V.VISKOVATOV — Translation by MARK CONRAD
SWU-800-006

UNIFORMS OF RUSSIAN ARMY DURING THE YEARS 1825-1855
VOL.07 - REIGN OF NICHOLAS I OF RUSSIA 1825-1855
GUARDS INFANTRY & GUARDS CUIRASSIERS REGIMENTS
A.V.VISKOVATOV — Translation by MARK CONRAD
SWU-800-007

IMPERIAL SOLDIERS & UNIFORMS 1640-1860
IN THE ART OF FRANZ GERASCH
LUCA S.CRISTINI — Plates by FRANZ GERASCH
SWU-GEN-001

UNIFORMS OF EUROPEAN ARMIES DURING THE BATAVIAN REVOLUTION
FROM THE AMSTERDAM CIVIC GUARD TO FOREIGN ARMIES: FRENCH, DUTCH, ENGLISH, AUSTRIAN, PRUSSIAN AND GERMAN STATES IN THE YEARS 1795-1787
LUCA STEFANO CRISTINI - J.D.LANGENDIJK - S.G.CASTEN
SWU-NAP-001

POLISH SOLDIERS DURING THE NAPOLEONIC WARS
THE POLISH LEGIONS, THE ARMY OF THE DUCHY OF WARSAW AND THE POLISH IN THE GRAND ARMÉE
LUCA STEFANO CRISTINI
SWU-NAP-002

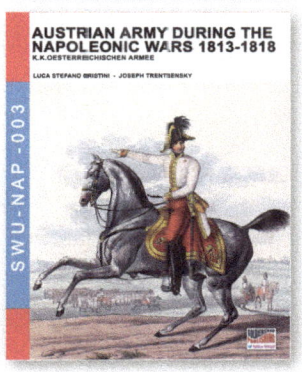

AUSTRIAN ARMY DURING THE NAPOLEONIC WARS 1813-1818
K.K.OESTERREICHISCHEN ARMEE
LUCA STEFANO CRISTINI - JOSEPH TRENTSENSKY
SWU-NAP-003

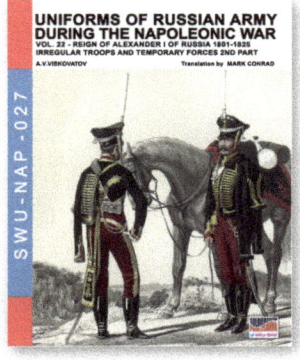

UNIFORMS OF RUSSIAN ARMY DURING THE NAPOLEONIC WAR
VOL. 22 - REIGN OF ALEXANDER I OF RUSSIA 1801-1825
IRREGULAR TROOPS AND TEMPORARY FORCES 2ND PART
A.V.VISKOVATOV — Translation by MARK CONRAD
SWU-NAP-027

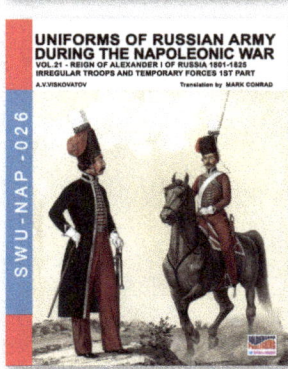

UNIFORMS OF RUSSIAN ARMY DURING THE NAPOLEONIC WAR
VOL.21 - REIGN OF ALEXANDER I OF RUSSIA 1801-1825
IRREGULAR TROOPS AND TEMPORARY FORCES 1ST PART
A.V.VISKOVATOV — Translation by MARK CONRAD
SWU-NAP-026

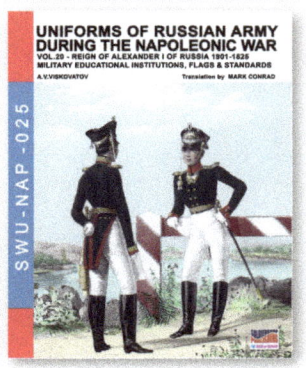

UNIFORMS OF RUSSIAN ARMY DURING THE NAPOLEONIC WAR
VOL.20 - REIGN OF ALEXANDER I OF RUSSIA 1801-1825
MILITARY EDUCATIONAL INSTITUTIONS, FLAGS & STANDARDS
A.V.VISKOVATOV — Translation by MARK CONRAD
SWU-NAP-025

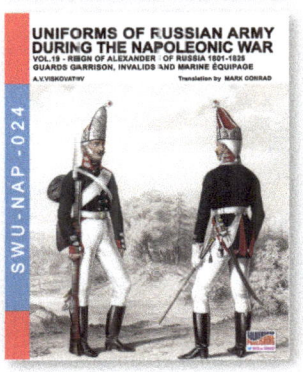

UNIFORMS OF RUSSIAN ARMY DURING THE NAPOLEONIC WAR
VOL.19 - REIGN OF ALEXANDER OF RUSSIA 1801-1825
GUARDS GARRISON, INVALIDS AND MARINE EQUIPAGE
A.V.VISKOVATOV — Translation by MARK CONRAD
SWU-NAP-024

UNIFORMS OF RUSSIAN ARMY DURING THE NAPOLEONIC WAR
VOL.18 - REIGN OF ALEXANDER I OF RUSSIA 1801-1825
GUARDS ARTILLERY, ENGINEERS & GENERAL STAFF
A.V.VISKOVATOV — Translation by MARK CONRAD
SWU-NAP-023

www.ingramcontent.com/pod-product-compliance
Lightning Source LLC
Chambersburg PA
CBHW041147120626
46547CB00020B/3142